CLASSROOM TO CAREER

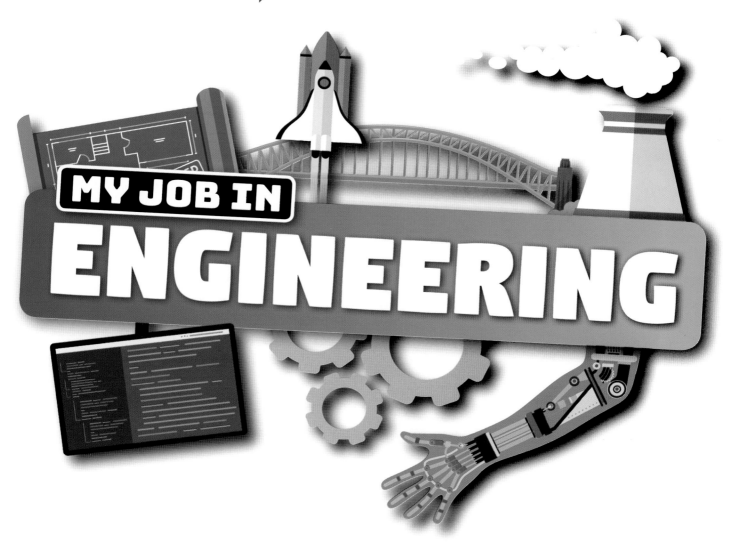

MY JOB IN
ENGINEERING

BY
JOANNA BRUNDLE

PowerKiDS
press ™

New York

Published in 2022 by The Rosen
Publishing Group, Inc.
29 East 21st Street, New York, NY 10010

© 2022 Booklife Publishing
This edition is published by arrangement
with Booklife Publishing

Edited by:
John Wood

Designed by:
Drue Rintoul

Cataloging-in-Publication Data

Names: Brundle, Joanna.
Title: My job in engineering / Joanna
Brundle.
Description: New York : PowerKids Press,
2022. | Series: Classroom to career |
Includes glossary and index.
Identifiers: ISBN 9781725336384 (pbk.)
| ISBN 9781725336407 (library bound) |
ISBN 9781725336391 (6 pack) |
ISBN 9781725336414 (ebook)
Subjects: LCSH: Engineering--Vocational
guidance--Juvenile literature.
Classification: LCC TA157.B767 2022 |
DDC 620.0023--dc23

Manufactured in the United
States of America

CPSIA Compliance Information: Batch #CWPK22.
For Further Information contact Rosen Publishing,
New York, New York at 1-800-237-9932.

Find us on

CONTENTS

WORDS THAT LOOK LIKE THIS CAN BE FOUND IN THE GLOSSARY ON PAGE 31.

CLASSROOM TO CAREER

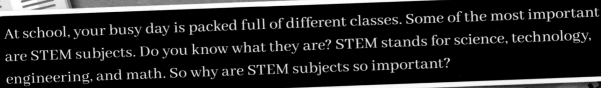

At school, your busy day is packed full of different classes. Some of the most important are STEM subjects. Do you know what they are? STEM stands for science, technology, engineering, and math. So why are STEM subjects so important?

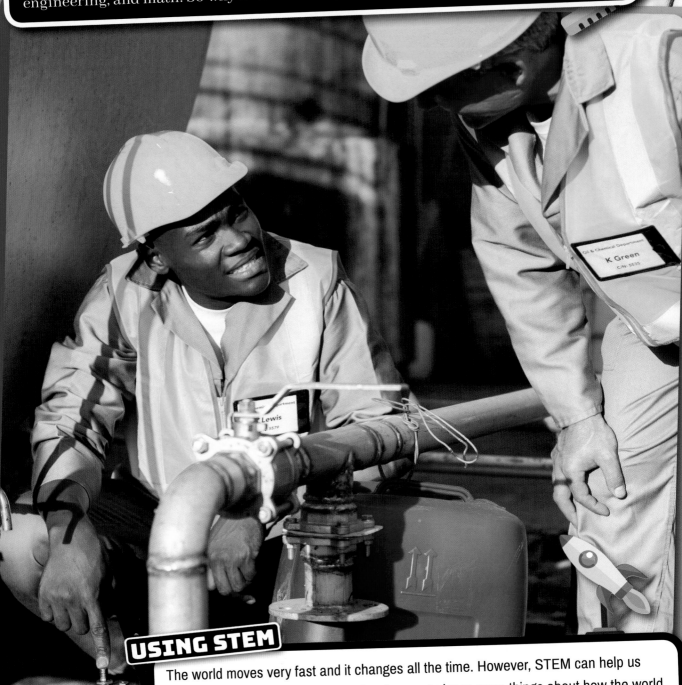

USING STEM

The world moves very fast and it changes all the time. However, STEM can help us understand it. STEM subjects can inspire you to learn more things about how the world works, and they might lead to you working in STEM. Lots of new STEM jobs are being created all the time and in lots of different areas. Who knows what you could be doing in the future? As well as helping you to find interesting work, studying STEM subjects will also help you to solve problems, make decisions, and work as part of a team.

JOB OR CAREER?

A job is something that you do to earn money. Many people stay in jobs for a short amount of time, and they don't always need training. A career is a lifelong work journey in an area that really interests you. People often need the right training for the right career.

Being a doctor is a lifelong career.

STEM subjects can help you get into an exciting career, whether you want to be a robotics engineer, a web designer, or an astronaut. But STEM subjects are important whatever you do. For example, many careers need you to have computer skills. In this book, we are going to look at engineering and the careers it might lead you to.

WHAT IS ENGINEERING?

Engineers use math and science to build and test equipment, machines, and structures. Examples of engineering include the vehicle that brought you to school and the machinery used to design and print this book.

Robotics engineer

AUTOMOTIVE ENGINEER

Are you crazy for cars or mad for motorcycles? Do you like the idea of designing and building the vehicles of the future? If so, a career as an automotive engineer could be for you.

Automotive engineers use clay models to work on design ideas.

Automotive engineers design and make all sorts of vehicles, such as buses, trucks, cars, and motorcycles. Using CAD (computer-aided design) programs, they design new vehicles and improve old ones. They make plans and drawings, work out the costs, and make <u>prototypes</u>. Prototypes are used to test how safe and strong the vehicle will be. Automotive engineers also choose the right materials for the project. They work out how it is going to be made and how all the components (which are the parts that make up the vehicle) will fit together.

An important part of the job is to keep up to date with modern ideas and to create vehicles that customers like and that meet their needs. Vehicles also have to follow rules made by the government about things such as safety, fuel, and <u>emissions</u>. You might design or improve safety features, such as air bags, or research better batteries for electric and <u>hybrid vehicles</u>. You will also make sure that high-quality vehicles are built. Costs and planning also have to be carefully managed, so that vehicles are made at the right price and on time.

Some automotive companies now only make electric vehicles.

To be an automotive engineer, you will need a college <u>degree</u> in automotive, mechanical, or manufacturing engineering. You will also need to be able to study data (information) to help you solve problems. It is important to be good at working in a team and explaining your work to customers and <u>colleagues</u>. Work experience is really important too, so pick a degree that offers ways of giving you that experience.

AEROSPACE ENGINEER

A career as an aerospace engineer might involve researching, designing, and testing all sorts of aerospace technology. These include passenger, cargo, or military airplanes, helicopters, spacecraft, and satellites.

Some aerospace engineers specialize in aircraft that fly in Earth's atmosphere. Others specialize in spacecraft that fly outside of Earth's atmosphere, such as rockets, space vehicles, and probes.

As an aerospace engineer, you could find yourself working for all sorts of employers, including airlines, governments, research organizations, or the armed forces. You might work for a national space agency, such as those found in the United States, the United Kingdom, China, and India. There is also the European Space Agency.

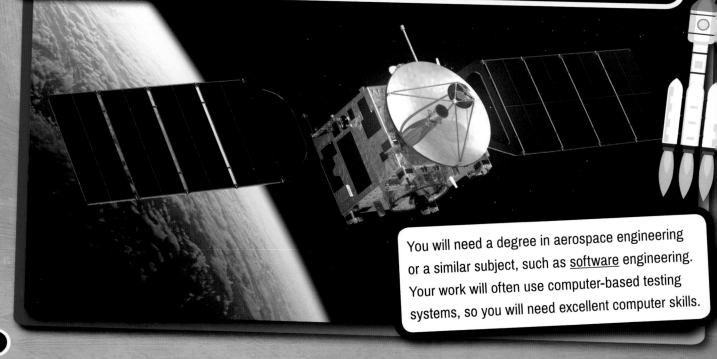

You will need a degree in aerospace engineering or a similar subject, such as software engineering. Your work will often use computer-based testing systems, so you will need excellent computer skills.

There are many roles within aerospace engineering. You might, for example, get involved in aerodynamics. This looks at the forces of lift (how an aircraft goes up) and drag (the force that slows an aircraft down as it moves through air). You could design engines, control systems, or the electrical systems used on the aircraft. An important part of the work is meeting customers to find out what they need. You will then help work out what the cost will be and when it can be done. Aerospace engineers are responsible for the safety of the finished vehicle, as well as how environmentally friendly it is.

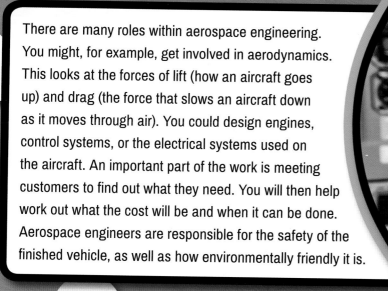

The cockpit of an aircraft is full of electronic equipment.

You are likely to spend most of your time working in an office or aerospace <u>laboratory</u>, where you will test and study <u>computer models</u> before any vehicles can be built. You may spend some of your time in a production <u>hangar</u>, where the vehicles are put together.

Engineers fixing an airplane

CIVIL ENGINEER

Have you ever traveled over a bridge high above a river or through a tunnel deep under the ocean? Did you wonder how these structures were built and how they stay in place? The answers lie in the work of a civil engineer.

London Stadium

Civil engineers build and repair structures and buildings. Examples of structures include railways, airports, sports arenas, roads, canals, power plants, water and <u>sewage</u> systems, flood barriers, pipelines, bridges, and tunnels. As a civil engineer you can follow a project from beginning to end, meaning that you get to see how the structure you have helped to create improves people's lives.

A consulting civil engineer plans and designs. A contracting civil engineer turns those designs into something real, making sure everything runs smoothly while building. They also make sure it is completed on time and at the right cost.

Sewer pipe

As a consulting civil engineer, you will carry out site investigations, think about possible problems, and use CAD programs to make detailed plans. As a contracting civil engineer, you will make sure that materials are available, and that the work is completed properly so that the customer is happy. Your work will also involve making sure that everyone is wearing the right safety equipment and working in a safe way. As well as working as part of a team involving <u>architects</u> and <u>sub-contractors</u>, you may also have to deal with complaints from people who are affected by the project.

Hard hats and other safety equipment must be worn on site.

If civil engineering is what you want to do, you will need a degree in civil or structural engineering. You could also become a civil engineer with an apprenticeship. In an apprenticeship, you are trained as you work on the job. At work, your time will be split between office-based tasks and site visits.

Civil engineers are often needed for projects in developing countries, such as this rail project in Bangladesh.

MINING ENGINEER

Mining means getting valuable metal, rocks, stones, and minerals out of the ground. People mine things such as aluminium and iron <u>ores</u>, gold, silver, tin, copper, coal, granite, diamonds, sapphires, emeralds, and rubies. As a mining engineer, your role will be to make sure things are removed safely and quickly.

The Cullinan diamond mine in South Africa has produced some of the biggest diamonds ever found.

Mining engineers check rock samples, waterways, and maps to decide if it is safe to set up a mine, and if it will make money. If so, they plan and design underground and surface mines. Underground mining involves building shafts and tunnels. If surface mines are used, mining engineers decide where pits should be dug and how to get rid of the rock and soil that is removed. Mining engineers train and manage teams of workers. They also make sure mines are closed safely when the work is finished.

Underground coal mine tunnel

Mining can be extremely dangerous. An important part of your work will be to make sure workers are safe and using the right equipment. You will inspect tunnels to make sure that they are properly supported and not in danger of collapsing. You will also make sure that there are ventila systems, so that workers are protected from poisonous gases. You might get involved in the use of explosives to blast rocks.

You will need a degree in mining, mineral engineering, or a similar subject, such as geology (the study of rocks). Mining engineers are needed all over the world, especiall in Australia, South America, and Africa.

Some mining engineers design or sell specialist mining equipment, such as rock cutters, conveyor belts, and underground railways.

Mining can cause pollution and environmental damage. For example, it can cause deforestation. Mining engineers are sometimes employed by environmental agencies to give advice on how to look after the environment while mining.

WATER ENGINEER

Water – we all need it to survive. But do you ever think about what happens to rain, where our water comes from when we turn on the tap, or where it goes when we use the toilet or take a shower?

Water engineers plan and build the structures and systems that give us clean water and get rid of wastewater and sewage. They also build and repair structures that control and store water. These include dams, reservoirs, and pumping stations, as well as flood defenses, such as sea walls and tidal barriers.

The Thames Barrier in London, UK, has ten gates that can be raised into position across the River Thames to protect the city from flooding.

Some water engineers are employed by environmental agencies, which are responsible for flood defenses and flood warning systems, as well as river and coastal defenses. Others work with environmental charities and with international charities that work to provide clean water, toilets, and hygiene for everyone.

The work of water engineers is likely to become more and more important due to climate change. Our planet is warming up, and there will be less and less water in some areas due to <u>evaporation</u>. Other areas will see more rainfall and storms. Melting polar ice will also raise sea levels, causing flooding. As a water engineer, your work might involve dealing with some of these problems.

If you care about global warming and are passionate about protecting the environment, this career in engineering might be perfect for you.

Polar ice melting

If you would like to be a water engineer, you will need a degree in a relevant subject, particularly civil, mechanical, or environmental engineering. Good IT skills are important, as you will use computer models to study things, such as the effects of flooding. You will also need to be good at writing reports and presenting your plans to other people.

MECHANICAL ENGINEER

Are you always taking things apart and then putting them back together? Do you like to see how they work or move and how all the parts fit together? If this sounds interesting, you might enjoy a career as a mechanical engineer.

Mechanical engineering is all about machines. Mechanical engineers research, build, and repair the components (parts) used in many types of machines. Most industries use mechanical systems, so there are lots of companies that employ mechanical engineers. A manufacturing company might employ you to work on buildings, vehicles, or aircraft. Some mechanical engineers work in transportation, health care, or the armed forces. Some work for energy companies that drill for oil or gas and control <u>refineries</u>. Wherever there are machines, mechanical engineers are involved.

Offshore oil and gas platform

The work of a mechanical engineer can be different each day. One day you might be planning a new project, working with a customer on the design and costs. Another day you might be testing how well components work. You will use CAD and CAM (computer-aided manufacturing) software to make your designs. You may have to check that machinery is running safely, and then fix any problems as quickly as possible. Your day might be spent in an office, a laboratory, or on site at a workshop or factory.

This mechanical engineer is using CAD software to design a new machine part.

In order to be a mechanical engineer, you will need a degree in mechanical engineering or a similar engineering subject, such as manufacturing engineering. Mechanical engineers are usually very good at math and science.

You will need to be good with computers and good at talking to people. Many employers offer internships or project work opportunities as part of your degree. This work experience is very helpful in finding full-time employment later.

MOTORSPORTS ENGINEER

Motorsports are filled with fast-paced, thrilling action. If you love cars and would like to work in this exciting world, a career as a motorsports engineer could be for you.

Motorsports engineers design, test, develop, build, and race motor vehicles of all types. These include rally cars, motorbikes, sports cars, and single-seat race cars, such as Formula 1 cars.

Formula 1 cars can reach speeds of around 240 miles per hour.

As a motorsports engineer, you will design vehicles that are fast, powerful, and safe. These designs are turned into prototypes using computer software. You will then test working models on the racetrack before production of the vehicle begins. There are strict rules in motorsports, covering everything from fuel, brakes, suspension, wheels, and tires, to the materials used and the total weight of the vehicle. Motorsports engineers must follow all of these rules so that their vehicles are allowed to race.

Race engineers are responsible for setting up vehicles for the race, according to the racetrack conditions. Some tracks, for example, call for straight-line speed, others for speed through bends. Race engineers also have to take weather conditions into account.

Slick tires have no grooves or treads and give maximum grip in dry weather conditions. Wet weather tires have grooves to channel water away.

Race engineers monitor how well the vehicle and its different parts are performing during the race. They use computer information to study, for example, engine speed and fuel. They discuss the race with the driver or rider before and after and can also give instructions to them and receive feedback during the race, using an intercom system.

Lots of people want a career in motorsports. As well as engineering and IT skills, you will also need determination and a passion for racing. Motorsports involves moving from racetrack to racetrack, so you must be happy to travel and be away from home for long periods of time. Formula 1 and other race series travel all around the world, so you will have the chance to see lots of different countries.

AGRICULTURAL ENGINEER

Do you love the countryside? Are you interested in farming and the environment? Are you into tractors? If so, you should think about a career as an agricultural engineer.

Agricultural engineers plan and help build the machinery used by environmental agencies, companies that care for grass sports fields, and in farming. This machinery includes combine harvesters, loaders, plows, crop-spraying equipment, dump trucks, and industrial lawn mowers.

Combine harvester

Grain silos

Agricultural engineers give advice to farmers and other businesses. They deal with <u>irrigation</u> and water drainage and look at ways to protect water and soil. They also advise how land can be used in ways that stop damage to the environment. Another important part of the job is to plan and oversee the building of farm structures, such as silos for storing grain and places for animals to be kept.

Some projects, such as the building of roads and railways, can cause serious environmental problems, including damage to the number of animals and to forests and other habitats. As an agricultural engineer, you might have to check to see how planned projects might affect the environment.

To be an agricultural engineer, you will need an agricultural, environmental, or mechanical engineering degree. Your working day will be spent in an office or workshop and carrying out site visits or fieldwork.

If you would like to work abroad, there are lots of chances to do so in agricultural engineering. You might work in a developing country, for example, advising local farmers on the best ways of growing crops. You might work with a charity or other organization offering emergency aid following a war or a natural disaster, such as a famine or earthquake.

Tractor factory

BIOMEDICAL ENGINEER

If you have ever been to a hospital, you will have noticed how much equipment is needed to <u>diagnose</u> and care for patients. Maybe you have had an x-ray or scan or seen an EKG machine – a piece of equipment used to test how well a patient's heart is beating.

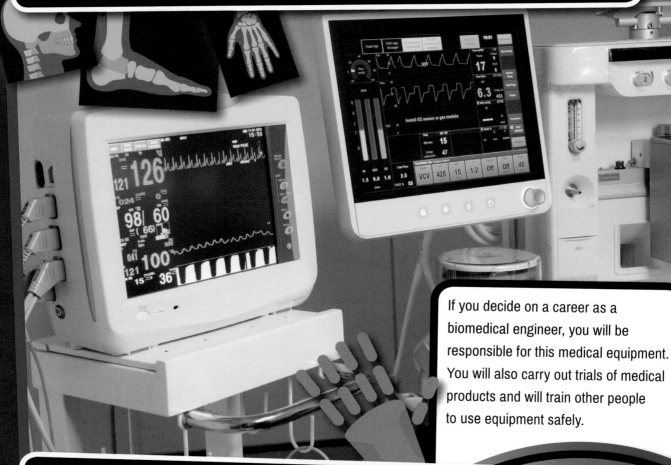

If you decide on a career as a biomedical engineer, you will be responsible for this medical equipment. You will also carry out trials of medical products and will train other people to use equipment safely.

Biomedical engineering joins together engineering and knowledge of the body to create groundbreaking and lifesaving products. These include <u>artificial</u> body parts, such as heart valves, artificial arms and legs, and equipment such as scanners, lasers, and robotic instruments. Biomedical engineers also design the computer software used to run medical equipment and test new drug treatments.

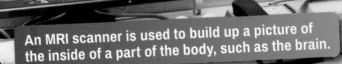
An MRI scanner is used to build up a picture of the inside of a part of the body, such as the brain.

Bioelectronic medicine is a new and exciting type of medicine for biomedical engineers. It involves designing small electronic devices that can be implanted inside the body and used to help healing or to treat conditions such as asthma. Biomedical engineers are also involved in tissue engineering. This involves growing tissue (the stuff bodies are made of) in the laboratory to repair or renew body parts.

You might prefer to work in <u>rehabilitation</u>. This involves making equipment and computer software for people who have suffered serious accidents or illnesses. The equipment helps them to recover and to live as normal a life as possible.

If you would like to work as a biomedical engineer, you will need to concentrate on STEM subjects at school. You will then need a degree in biomedical engineering or biomedical sciences. You could work for lots of different employers, such as hospitals, health and rehabilitation charities, and research organizations.

This hoist is used to lift the patient into his wheelchair.

ROBOTICS ENGINEER

You may think of a robot as belonging in a futuristic film or video game. Robots are, in fact, part of our everyday lives. They do all sorts of things, from packaging food to building and painting vehicles. In hospitals, robots perform surgery and robotic patients can be used to help train new doctors and nurses.

At home, robotic vacuum cleaners help with household jobs. The police and armed forces use robots to investigate suspected bombs or other dangers. Robots are also used to look at problems with underground sewers, and to move things around in warehouses and ports.

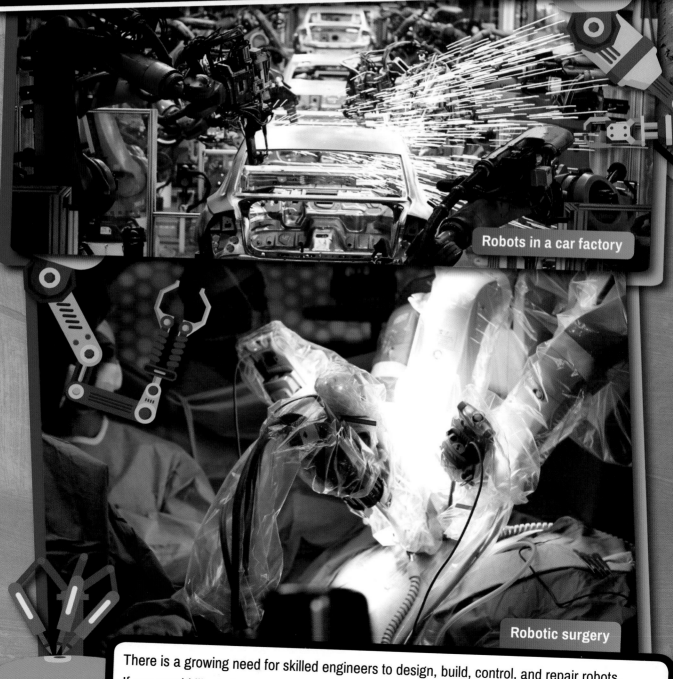

Robots in a car factory

Robotic surgery

There is a growing need for skilled engineers to design, build, control, and repair robots. If you would like to be part of this fast-moving world, robotics engineering is the career for you.

As a robotics engineer, you will design robots and work out how they will be built. You will also design the computer software used to control robots. Robots carry out many tasks that humans either cannot do or choose not to do because they are dangerous or boring. Your work as a robotics engineer will make those tasks easier, faster, and safer.

There are many interesting roles for robotics engineers. You might get involved in designing robotic toys. You might build robots for film studios and theme parks. Some robotics engineers make robots that are used to explore places that are hard for humans to get to, such as the deepest oceans or other planets.

The surface of Mars has been safely explored using robotic vehicles.

You will need a degree in robotics engineering, mechanical engineering, or mathematics. You will also need good computer skills, as you will be using CAD and CAM programs. Your working day will be split between the office and the laboratory, where you will work on the different parts needed to build the robots you have designed.

Animatronics are robots that are designed to look lifelike and behave in a lifelike manner.

MARINE ENGINEER

Do you enjoy being in, on, and around boats? Do you like the idea of working on the coast or at sea? If you are also good at math, science, and design, you could be a marine engineer. Marine engineers are involved with safely transporting things across the world on ships. They also work on projects on vehicles such as submarines.

Marine engineers design, control, and repair all the mechanical equipment on board a boat or ship. They often work closely with naval architects (boat designers) and other engineers to design and build all types of boat. These include sailboats, fishing boats, luxury yachts, ships, cruise ships, oil tankers, and aircraft carriers. Marine engineers may also be part of a team involved in the design and building of offshore wind farms.

Offshore wind farm

An aircraft carrier has a runway that allows military aircraft to take off and land.

Some of your work will be done in an office, where you will use CAD software. You will also need to go to sea to check and repair machinery. As a marine engineer, you will be responsible for all the systems on board a ship, such as the <u>navigation</u>, steering, electrical, <u>propulsion,</u> and engine systems. You will inspect marine machinery and equipment and carry out testing to make sure that it is working correctly and follows the rules that make it safe to use.

Ship's engine room

You will need a degree in marine engineering or a similar subject such as ocean engineering. You will also need to be good at working in a team. Most marine engineers choose to specialize in a particular area or type of vessel, for example oil, gas, or chemical tankers. Once you are fully trained and have experience, opportunities are available for marine engineers all over the world.

Oil and chemical tanker

ELECTRICAL ENGINEER

If you have ever had a power outage, either at home or school, you will understand how much we all rely on electricity every day. Without it, we cannot switch on a light, watch TV, or charge our phones and tablets.

Electrical engineers are responsible for bringing electricity safely into our homes and businesses. They research, design, and test electrical systems and equipment. There is a huge range of roles for electrical engineers. They might design electrical systems, such as wiring, lighting, and heating for homes or businesses. They also work on projects such as new power stations and railway or highway networks.

Control room at a power station

Electrical engineers often work on large-scale projects. Electronics and microelectronics engineers design and develop software and the tiny electrical parts and circuits used in computers and mobile devices, such as smartphones.

As an electrical engineer, you might work on the design of electrical systems for a new hospital, school, stadium, theme park, or shopping center. You could be involved in the design and manufacture of specialist medical equipment, such as scanners and robotic equipment. Aerospace projects, including the design of electrical systems for aircraft or spacecraft, also require electrical engineers. In fact, anywhere electricity is needed, electrical engineers are needed too!

In order to work as an electrical engineer, you will need a degree in electrical or electronics engineering or in a similar subject, such as a science subject. On large-scale projects, you will need to work in a team. You may work in an office, workshop, laboratory, or factory.

There are plenty of opportunities for electrical and electronics engineers to work abroad, particularly for oil and gas companies, large construction companies, and research organizations.

ENGINEERS WHO HAVE CHANGED THE WORLD

LEONARDO DA VINCI

Leonardo da Vinci came up with ideas for engineering projects that were way ahead of his time and led to the invention of things such as the submarine, parachute, helicopter, tank, and diving suit. He also produced very early designs for canals, bridges, churches, flying machines, and even the first robot.

ELLEN OCHOA

Ellen Ochoa used to be an astronaut for NASA. She helped to invent machines that help scientists to see images that come from space more clearly.

ARCHIMEDES

Archimedes was one of the most important engineers of all time. He is famous for inventing the Archimedes screw, which uses a screw in a pipe to raise water from one level to another.

SARAH GUPPY

At a time when women were not given a fair chance to be engineers, Sarah Guppy created a design in 1811 for building suspension bridges. Her ideas led to the building of the Clifton Suspension Bridge.

GLOSSARY

architects	people who design buildings and supervise their construction
artificial	something that is made by humans and is not natural
atmosphere	the mixture of gases that make up the air and surround Earth
colleagues	a group of people who work together
computer models	programs created on computers to test real-life situations
deforestation	the clearing of forests to make way for agriculture, construction, or mining
degree	a qualification in a specialist subject, often given by a university or college to people usually over the age of 18
diagnose	examine a patient's symptoms to find out what is wrong with them
emissions	substances, especially pollutants, sent out into the air by an engine
environmental agencies	organizations that protect, manage, and conserve the natural world
evaporation	the process by which a liquid turns into a gas, due to increased heat or pressure
hangar	a building with a very large floor area, used for building or storing aircraft
hybrid vehicles	vehicles that use two different forms of power, for example a gas engine and an electric motor
irrigation	the artificial supply of water to crops to help them grow
laboratory	a room or building used to carry out experiments or research
national space agency	an organization that develops space programs for their nation. Many of these organizations work together at an international level.
navigation	the process of planning and following a route
ores	naturally occurring solid materials, such as rocks, that contain valuable metals and minerals
organizations	groups, companies, or businesses
probes	small, unmanned spacecraft sent into space to gather information and send it back to scientists on Earth
propulsion	the force that pushes something forward
prototypes	first versions of a product from which other improved versions are developed
refineries	factories where products in their natural state, such as oil, are made pure or converted into valuable products
rehabilitation	the process of returning someone to health or normal life using training and therapies
satellites	machines sent into space to orbit planets, take photographs, and collect and send information
sewage	a system by which wastewater is carried away and made harmless
software	the programs or instructions that tell a computer how to work
sub-contractors	people or companies that are hired to carry out particular tasks as part of a larger project
technology	devices or tools to help us do something
ventilation	the movement of fresh air around an enclosed space or the system that does this

INDEX

Photo Credits

Images are courtesy of Shutterstock.com. With thanks to Getty Images, Thinkstock Photo and iStockphoto.
2&3 – VitalyVK. 4&5 – michaeljung, SofikoS, Chutima Chaochaiya. 6&7 – Monkey Business Images, Pavel L Photo and Video, Placid Gorilla, buffaloboy, Macrovector, VectorShow. 8&9 – Ewa Studio, 3Dsculptor, Media_works, Sebastian stocking, Oleg and Polly, VikiVector, Meilun, Truevector, notbad. 10&11 – Rob Wilson, kitzcorner, Kzenon, Md Azmir Hossen, VectorPot, Pogorelova Olga, Meilun, Gvais. 12&13 – Angela N Perryman, Marianna Ianovska, Mark Agnor, JVrublevskaya, Macrovector, Rvector, ideyweb. 14&15 – Marc Pinter, Magsi, Bernhard Staehli. Have a nice day Photo, Marnikus, 4zevar, THAWEESAK NAMMANEEWONG, Sudowoodo, solar22. 16&17 – fuyu liu, curraheeshutter. Monkey Business Images, Stokkete, MSSA. 18&19 – Four Oaks, Ev. Safronov, navee sangvitoon, Magicleaf, Maksim M, NaughtyNut. 20&21 – My Portfolio, Deyana Stefanova Robova, Grigvovan, Maksim Safaniuk, Anatolir, aShatilov, Beresnev. 22&23 – nimon, Image Supply, Pressmaster, belushi, RedlineVector, Anatolir, Zentangle, Amanita Silvicora. 24&25 – Jenson, Master Video, Triff, kateafter, Multigon, Solveig Been, studioworkstock, VectorPlotnikoff, VectorSun. 26&27 – Vadim Petrakov, temp-64GTX, tantawat, StockStudio Aerials, MicroOne, Marnikus. 28&29 – Suwin, Leonardo da, Racheal Grazias, Oil and Gas Photographer, hvostik, edel. 30 – Everett Historical, A.Sych, stocker1970.